A Guide to Project Auditing

Association for Project Management

Association for Project Management
Ibis House, Regent Park
Summerleys Road, Princes Risborough
Buckinghamshire
HP27 9LE

British Library Cataloguing in Publication Data is available.
Paperback ISBN: 978-1-903494-74-5
eISBN: 978-1-903494-75-2

Cover design by Fountainhead Creative Consultants
Typeset by RefineCatch Limited, Bungay, Suffolk
in 10/14pt Foundry Sans

Contents

Acknowledgements

The guide was prepared by members of the APM's Assurance SIG led by Roy Millard as chair. The authors of the guide are Peter Deary, Mushtaq Ali and Mark Reilly.

The authors acknowledge the contributions of Pascal Barras, Wendy Gregory, Tony Hargraves, Julian Harris, Chris Little, Gary Poole, Nicola Read, Pauline Scott and Naveed Sheikh in the preparation of the guide.

1

Introduction

1.1 Introduction

Project assurance is a fundamental part of effective project governance. The project audit is the means to provide that assurance and enables the sponsor to have confidence that the governance is working and that the project is being managed as intended. There is currently a considerable amount of information relating to the assurance of projects and programmes, and why it is important. This guide seeks to demonstrate how to plan and undertake a comprehensive audit of a project, thereby providing that assurance.

The guide seeks to explain the role of an audit, how it could be planned and undertaken, the degrees of assurance that can be given, and how project audits can be aligned to organisational governance. Although the guide acknowledges the need for project audits to be integrated with the works of other assurance providers (particularly technical and quality audits) a project audit is a stand-alone process aimed at the three main roles involved in a project.

The three main roles involved in project audits are:

Role	Description
Organisation board/audit committee/sponsor/other stakeholders	Those who schedule the project audit and receive the audit findings
Project team	Those whose project is being audited, with whom the auditors interact
Project auditor(s)	Those who undertake the audit, and report its findings and make recommendations

For any audit to be successful and provide value to all parties, these three main roles must work together and understand each other's function in the process.

As is common in all projects it is vital that there is a recognition that people undertaking different project roles may have differing interests and perceptions about project outputs, progress and the various stakeholders. This guide therefore refers to how audits relate to the various responsibilities within a project and how to apply the processes associated with auditing in a project context taking project responsibilities into consideration. These processes include: the development of an annual audit plan; choosing the auditor/audit team to undertake the work; developing an audit programme; performing, closing, and reporting the audit; and undertaking follow-ups.

1.2 Purpose of the guide

This guide is principally intended for use by project auditors in developing an audit approach to the review and assurance of projects. However, it is also intended to be of value to anyone involved in the management and administration of projects, as it records areas of project risk, and identifies audit evidence and practices. The guide will also indicate those aspects of a project which the auditors may choose to review, and how the audit will be performed.

 This guide is not intended to provide step-by-step instructions on how to carry out audits on any particular type of project; rather, it will provide guidance which can be adapted by the user to the circumstances of their own projects. The audit can then be planned, performed and reported on, and based on the auditor's preferred approach, adapted to suit the particular project discipline.

 In section 2.2.1, and expanded in Appendix 1, the guide proposes some elements and areas of interest for review by project auditors, together with the risks and expected controls to manage those risks. These elements do not form an exhaustive list so it is recommended that further assessment by the project auditor is always necessary to decide upon areas of focus before a project audit is undertaken.

1.3 Structure of the guide

The guide focuses on the various aspects of project audits, to answer the following three questions:

- **What is an audit?** (And how an audit differs from other assurance methods.)
- **Why do we undertake project audits?**
- **How should a project audit be planned, performed, evaluated, reported, and followed up?**

This guide covers the planning of project audits (Section 2.1); suggested elements of a project which are to be reviewed (Section 2.2.1 and Appendix 1); evaluation and reporting (Section 2.3); and follow-up processes (Section 2.4).

1.4 What is project auditing?

Auditing is defined by the Chartered Institute of Internal Auditors as 'an independent, objective assurance and consulting activity designed to add value and improve an organisation's operations. It helps an organisation accomplish its objectives by bringing a systematic, disciplined approach to evaluate and improve the effectiveness of risk management, control, and governance processes'.

In any audit, the auditor(s) perceives and recognises the propositions before them for examination, collects evidence, evaluates the same, and on this basis formulates an opinion on the adequacy of controls within the activity being audited.

Throughout this guide we use the term 'project' to mean 'a unique, transient endeavour undertaken to achieve planned objectives' (see APM *Body of Knowledge,* 6th edition); the audit of programmes and portfolios will require different techniques. Auditing of a project should be seen in the context of the definition of project, programme and portfolio (P3) assurance set out in the APM *Body of Knowledge*: P3 Assurance is 'the process of providing confidence to stakeholders that projects, programmes and portfolios will achieve their scope, time, cost and quality objectives, and realise their benefits'.

1.5 Principles of project audit

The APM publication *A Guide to Integrated Assurance* identifies the principles governing project audit, which are those established for the provision of assurance generally. Project audit should be:

- independent, and supported in this by the organisation board;
- accountable within a governance and reporting system;
- planned and coordinated as part of the organisation's management system;
- proportionate to risk potential and the assurance needs of stakeholders;
- risk-based, against an independent risk evaluation;
- able to allow the impact of identified weaknesses to be reported and addressed, by follow-up and escalation.

1.6 Project life cycle

The APM *Body of Knowledge* identifies four, and where appropriate five, phases of a project life cycle:

- **Concept**: an initial idea is developed through production of an outline business case and schedule. At this stage a project sponsor is appointed to lead development of the idea, and to provide the answer to two questions:
  - Is the project likely to be viable?
  - Is it definitely worth investing in the next, definition phase?
- **Definition**: the preferred solution is identified and ways of achieving this are refined. The project management plan (PMP) is developed. Approval of this and the business case must be given by the sponsor before progressing to the development phase.
- **Development**: the PMP is put into action. The continuing viability of the project may be assessed and reviewed at various stages throughout this phase.
- **Handover and closure**: the project outputs are handed over and accepted by the sponsor on behalf of the users.
- Where appropriate, **Benefits realisation**: a project may include a benefits realisation phase.

Throughout the phases of a project there should be provision for independent audit to give assurance to key stakeholders including the project sponsor and executive board, of the likelihood that the objectives of the project will be achieved.

1.7 Why do we need project audits?

The giving of assurance to project stakeholders, including the organisation board, through providing assessment of the likelihood of the project achieving its objectives, is a fundamental aspect of project governance (see APM guides: *Directing Change – A Guide to Governance of Project Management*, and *A Guide to Integrated Assurance*). This assurance will cover the identification and management of risk, evaluation of opportunities, and actions being taken to realise those benefits on which approval of the business case was based. Assurance also seeks evidence of effective controls and opportunities to increase the likelihood of success of the project. The audit will consider among other things the following elements (see also 2.2.1 below):

- project definition and requirements management;
- project organisation and governance;
- risks management;
- commercial, procurement and commissioning;
- configuration management, project change controls and the PMO;
- project planning and scheduling;
- performance and benefits management;
- stakeholder management and communications;
- organisational capability and culture;
- social responsibility and sustainability.

1.8 Who should use the guide?

1.8.1 The project sponsor

The sponsor must ensure that their projects or programmes meet the organisational requirements. The sponsor can use the audit function to assist them in meeting these needs by understanding the scope of audits available to them, and by selecting specific audits that address the projects' risks and also take into consideration the position in the project life cycle.

In relation to audits they are responsible for liaising with the audit team in planning a programme of project audits; providing support to the audit team; and ensuring that remedial actions are implemented.

1.8.2 The project team

Delivery of the project and of its ability to achieve the expected outputs and outcomes is the responsibility of the project team. In doing this the project is expected to provide assurance and comfort to the wider organisation that it is being delivered in a structured and controlled manner and in accordance with organisation protocols including controls, systems and procedures. Project audits are a principal way for organisations to review and assess that their projects, programmes and portfolios will deliver the expected outcomes and benefits.

In relation to audits, the project team is responsible for ensuring data, information and staff are available to participate in the audit; responding to audit findings; and resolving any issues arising.

1.8.3 The project auditor

The auditor is not only responsible for undertaking the audit and reporting the findings. They also undertake a key role in working with the sponsor and project community in the management, communication and scheduling of audits across the organisation.

The responsibilities of the auditor in relation to the audits include identifying the risks to be reviewed; planning and carrying out the audit; and reporting to the project sponsor on findings made and overall rating of the audit as defined by the organisation's audit function.

2

Project audit process

In terms of auditing techniques, a project audit is no different from any other form of risk-based or compliance audit. However, unlike other types of audit, the range of topics, disciplines and risks to consider for audit can be wide-ranging. Without careful planning, the scope of a project audit can become too broad to manage or lack sufficient depth to find the real issues. As a result, auditing a project may be broken down into several audits (each with a distinct purpose) over the lifetime of a project. Auditors with a specialist background/discipline may be engaged at different stages e.g. an engineer to audit the design elements of the project; an environmentalist to cover environmental compliance and sustainability; a health and safety expert to see that facility design and construction is safe, etc. Such experts may come from different audit and assurance providers within/outside the organisation. The challenge for the organisation (and the project sponsor) may then be to manage and integrate (see APM: *A Guide to Integrated Assurance*) all of these audit interventions to ensure that the project is not overwhelmed, there is no duplication and each audit adds value.

Based on APM's five phases of the project life cycle (concept; definition; development; handover and close; and if required, benefits realisation) the current phase of the project should be determined prior to starting the audit as this will allow the auditor to focus the audit programme/questions to the priority areas of the project. During the project audit, various project areas will be assessed to ensure adequate controls are in place. These project areas change in priority throughout the project life cycle. For example, the priority of assessing controls for developing the business case development is higher at Concept stage than it would be at the Handover and Close phase, and the priority of assessing the controls around project closure would be lower in the Concept phase than it will be at the Handover and Close phase.

2.1 Planning the audit

2.1.1 Audit prioritisation

Project audits should be prioritised within the context of the organisation's annual audit plan and the requirements of its audit committee. Project audits should be planned on the basis of risks to the organisation and to the project.

2.1.2 Choosing the audit team

Conducting a project audit is a specialist skill, so at least one influential member of the audit team should have knowledge and experience of a project environment. The size of the team should be appropriate to the scale and risks faced by the project and the requirements of the audit programme. Most organisations which are developing projects will have access to this skillset, which need not necessarily be held by an experienced auditor; such people could be managed by an experienced audit supervisor. The audit team should have access to specialist technical skills e.g. quality assurance, and should bear in mind the organisation's appetite for integrated assurance.

2.1.3 Information gathering

This table below is an example of a format that could be used to record relevant information for the audit. The list is not exhaustive and can be amended or adapted:

	Background information	Results
1	Project name/reference	
2	Brief description of the objectives of the project and any relevant notes. Record any information here that will help in assessing risk areas for audit	
3	Project value (total)/(this year)	
4	Appropriate (outline or full) business case approved/date/value	
5	Agreed project audit scope, objectives and name/reference	
6	Project governance arrangements including project sponsor, project manager and project team	
7	Project management arrangements	

8	Project phase (Inception, Feasibility, Development, Delivery, Close-out)	
9	Overview of project controls including change controls	
10	Project Management Plan (PMP) and Project Initiation Document (PID) approved date	
11	Project audit team details	
12	Organisation policies and procedures to be used as basis for project audit	
13	Extent of PMO support required including management, cost and financial reports	
14	Risks from corporate and project risk registers, and additional risks from discussion with stakeholders	
15	Project and organisation risk management and mitigation measures	
16	Integration with other assurance providers	
17	Alignment of project with corporate strategy	
18	Risk-based audit programme and schedule	
19	Audit reporting details including timetable	
20	Significant stakeholders (including their influence and interest)	
21	Communications strategy	
22	Arrangements to hand over to next phase, stage or client of project	

2.1.4 Risk assessing a project

The project risk register should be used as the basis of planning a project audit. The risk register should be consistent with the organisation's own risk register and its risk and opportunity appetite. This should be enhanced by discussion with stakeholders on risks they have identified but which have not been included in the formal register; and on the auditor's own experience and discussion with the project team.

2.1.5 The project audit programme

The project audit programme should be based on the audit scope and objectives, agreed with the sponsor, or the organisation's audit committee. The audit team should identify the risks to the project, and the controls and tests which are derived from these. The different phases of the project life cycle should lead to audit programmes and tests appropriate to those phases, and to the nature of the project.

2.2 Fieldwork

The audit team should gather information and documentation, and talk to key stakeholders including (as appropriate) members of the project team, the procurement function and the supply chain. There should be an effective working relationship with the project management office (PMO), to ensure that information, documents and reports are readily available for purposes of the audit, including the procedures and policies which form the basis of evaluation.

2.2.1 Elements for review

The APM publication, *Measures for Assuring Projects: APM Toolkit*, identifies 10 key categories of criteria for review, around which the project assurance process should be based. We have drawn on those categories stated within the toolkit, as offering guidance to the identification of elements for review in carrying out an audit of a project. In Appendix 1 this guide suggests some aspects of those elements, together with the associated risks and controls, which could be subject to audit review where appropriate. In Appendix 2 we have mapped across from those elements we have identified for project audit and review, to the toolkit's categories for which assurance should be sought. The selection of elements is not intended to be exhaustive, nor to serve as a project audit checklist; and it is expected that this should be adapted to reflect the circumstances of the project. The elements which have been identified are:

1. Project definition and requirements management – clear and controlled baseline requirements, objectives, success criteria, business case, terms of reference, contracts and benefits realisation.
2. Project organisation and governance – the processes to align the interests and strategic direction of sponsors and stakeholders.
3. Risks management – management of risks and opportunities through the life cycle of the project.
4. Commercial, procurement and commissioning – procurement and contract management, financial controls and engagement with commissioning processes.

5. Configuration management, project change controls and PMO – processes and systems to administer and control the project and changes to it.
6. Project planning and scheduling – appropriately detailed execution strategies, plans and schedules.
7. Performance and benefits management – to provide assurance that the benefits stated in the business case can be delivered within the resources made available.
8. Stakeholder management and communications – all stakeholders affected by the project have been identified and are appropriately involved.
9. Organisational capability and culture – people, behaviours, teams and the working environment including the organisation's culture.
10. Social responsibility and sustainability – managing the impact of project delivery on the social, physical, ecological and economic environment including health and safety.

2.3 Evaluation and reporting

In concluding the audit, the project will need to be evaluated against a clear set of criteria which the organisation expects. It will enable the sponsor to assess the likelihood of a successful outcome from the project and to develop a clear set of actions to address any matters going forward.

Provision of assurance covers not only the investigation and reporting of findings, but also includes the identification and implementation of actions to address those findings. The auditor will need to assess the findings made and how critical these are to success of the project and risk to the organisation.

Reporting requirements will vary between and within organisations and projects, but a sound and useful technique is to rate the findings in accordance with the agreed criteria, and to provide an overall evaluation score for the project. Such clear criteria offer benefits to the sponsor, and the audit and project teams in that consistency and rigour of approach will support objectivity in the audit process.

2.3.1 Evaluation

The overall evaluation of the project will often be directed towards the project sponsor, and the requirement to address the individual issues will be held within the project team.

The number of issues identified and their ratings will then determine the overall rating given to the project. There are numerous methods to rate findings and evaluate projects, but the basic idea is to use a grading score to rank each audited element and indicate the extent to which the project has performed.

One method of grading used extensively to measure performance is the 'traffic light' system of three ratings: red/amber/green (RAG). During project audits it may be more appropriate to use four or five ratings, with additional definitions and next steps. Definitions of RAG will depend on project and reporting requirements; the traffic light technique is used by many assurance providers and can be tied to reporting of the achievement of key performance indicators (KPIs). One definition of the ratings is:

- **Red:** there are significant issues with the project (such as tolerances set by the board for cost, time or quality have been exceeded). The matter should be escalated to the sponsor and project board immediately.
- **Amber:** a problem has had a negative effect on project performance but can be dealt with by the project team. One aspect of project viability is at risk but is within agreed tolerances. The sponsor and project board should be notified.
- **Green:** the project is performing to plan. All aspects of project performance are within tolerance. No action is needed.

2.3.2 Reporting

Individual organisations have their own reporting requirements, including who should receive the report, who has responsibility for responding to it and to what timescale, and who will be tasked with implementing its findings and recommendations. Provision should be made to issue the report in line with the agreed timetable, or sooner if circumstances require this. As some of the content of the report may be commercially or otherwise sensitive, this should be borne in mind in circulation and distribution of draft and final reports.

Following a close-out meeting with auditees, the preliminary report should be prepared and internally reviewed before issue to those auditees and other stakeholders for comment on findings and recommendations.

Importantly, responses may indicate that the organisation is willing to accept a degree of project risk greater than that on which the audit was based.

The final report, which should contain the evaluation rating based on the responses received, should be distributed in accordance with the requirements of the agreed audit plan. The final report should also be issued to the organisation's audit committee.

2.4 Follow-up

Follow-up is the final element of the audit process, in which the audit team confirms that the sponsor and project team have implemented the agreed actions to address identified project risks and issues. This can be confirmed by monitoring the implementation process, or by accepting a formal statement from the sponsor or project team that the recommended actions have been carried out.

2.5 Benefits evaluation

Where the scope of the project audit included evaluation or auditing of outcomes on which approval of the business case was based (the benefits realisation phase of the project life cycle), a separate audit process will be required. This will seek to compare recorded benefit outcomes against those proposed in the business case through the use of defined benefit measures, normally by quantitative methods. The organisation should normally have a benefits evaluation process by which it is able to carry out such evaluation itself without instructing the audit team to do so.

2.6 Legacy and lessons learned

The organisation may operate a legacy programme, to capture the intellectual capital within a project before the project team is disbanded. A notable example is the Learning Legacy programme developed by the 2012 Olympic Delivery Authority: this is open to everyone, to share knowledge of construction and event organisation. The results of project audits can provide valuable reference points for the organisation's legacy and lessons learned process. The audit team should be aware of the organisation's requirements for confidentiality if involved in the legacy and lessons learned process.

Appendix 1

Matrix of element-based areas of review, risks and controls

Element 1. Project definition and requirements management: clear and controlled baseline requirements, objectives, success criteria, business case, terms of reference, contracts and benefits realisation

Area of review	Risk	Control	Audit methods include
Business plan alignment	The programme/project is not aligned with organisation or business strategy	Formal approval of project start-up recorded and confirmation that it aligns with strategic objectives	Review of appropriate board minutes and documentation Review of stage gate (gateway) approvals Schedule of delegated authority
Business case	The business case is not robust, or does not exist or outputs and outcomes are not measurable	Senior responsible owner/sponsor identified with appropriate authority to deliver project outcomes	Review of approved business case to identify responsibilities and ensure that business case template and guidance is available
	Business case does not fit with organisation's model e.g. five case model: strategic, economic, commercial, financial and management cases	Requirement that business cases take account of approved model	Review of approved business case to assess extent of compliance
	Project cost as stated is not defined effectively or is insufficient to allow delivery If already funded: Level of agreed funding is insufficient to deliver objectives	Costs (including life cycle costs) have been reliably estimated and a mechanism exists for these to be refined Due account is taken of optimism bias in respect of cost	Review of cost methodology and processes based on approved business case Review of approved business case. Ensure that cost of risk has been accounted for Review whether additional funding should be sought to enable successful delivery

Area of review	Risk	Control	Audit methods include
	Target dates are unrealistic or overly ambitious	Target dates have been subject to a reality check and a mechanism exists for these dates to be refined Due account is taken of optimism bias in respect of target dates and schedules	Review of schedule and programme methodology and processes Review of approved business case
	Business cases are not used as a control against achievement of the project deliverables	Approved business case is used as a change control baseline document, and is subject to periodic review	Assessment of change control mechanisms applicable to project and that business case is routinely updated
Scope defined including change control processes	The project scope/requirements is not clearly defined or understood	Project scope defined Change control processes implemented Project manager's responsibilities and limits of authority defined	Review of approved business case – scope must be clear and unambiguous Assessment of change control processes Schedule of delegation in PID or approved business case
Requirements definition – clear/complete/understood? Required outcomes clear/agreed	The project's scope/plan is not baselined at time of project start	Project plan developed to appropriate level	Review of PID and approved business case to ensure clarity of scope and planning
Authorisation including definition of baseline	The project has commenced prior to formal authorisation	Project governance arrangements reflect organisation requirements	Review of project governance arrangements including authorisation to start projects

Area of review	Risk	Control	Audit methods include
Documenting client objectives and requirements and success criteria	Project deliverables and outcomes and what will represent success have not been identified or cannot be measured	Clear and unambiguous deliverables and objectives set out in PID and PMP Agreed outcomes and success criteria	Review of PID and PMP to ensure clarity and consistency with approved business case Review measurement criteria
Defining and managing expected benefits	Projects are undertaken without expected benefits being managed	Business case contains stated and quantified benefits Realisation of benefits is controlled by established processes	Review of approved business case to ensure benefits are stated Review of processes to ensure benefits can be baselined, controlled and can be measured
Agreeing and documenting acceptance process	Unclear acceptance processes	Documented acceptance processes for project and its elements Contractual controls available for implementation as needed	Review of PID and project governance to ensure clear acceptance processes exist
Readiness for acceptance and implementation of project	Commissioning processes and resources are not adequate to accept and deliver project benefits	Commissioning plans and processes are agreed in advance Sufficient resources are available for commissioning and change	Review of commissioning plans to ensure consistency with approved business case and benefits management processes Review resourcing and equipment planning Review measures in place for embedding benefits (if relating to change management)

Element 2. Project organisation and governance: the processes to align the interests and strategic direction of sponsors and stakeholders

Area of review	Risk	Control	Audit methods include
Project governance structures	Inadequate project governance structures or organisation inexperienced at implementing governance	Defined project governance structures based on organisation and project requirements Project sponsor appointed with appropriate authority to allocate resources and reinforce governance best practice	Review project governance arrangements to ensure consistency with organisation governance Terms of reference for project/programme boards Review organisation schedule of delegation
Sponsorship	The project sponsor is not an effective link between the organisation and project management	Ownership of business case and accountability for delivery are approved at organisation board level	Ensure role of sponsor is supported by organisation/board governance structures and are recorded in PID Evidence that there is buy-in to this process
Roles and responsibilities	Inadequately defined roles and responsibilities	Defined roles and responsibilities within a formal project and organisation management structure	Ensure roles and responsibilities are defined within a formal project and organisation governance and management structure and are recorded in the PID
Authorisation and approvals	Decisions and authorisations are made without proper authority or are made at a level unsuited to the requirements of effective project control	Approvals and authorisation processes are defined and are based on organisation and project requirements	Ensure approval and authorisation processes are defined within a formal project and organisation governance and management structure and are recorded in the PID Ensure that processes are being adhered to and that appropriate recording of decisions is in place

Area of review	Risk	Control	Audit methods include
Organisational structure	Project staffing and resource structures are unsuited to effective project management	Project structure reflects requirements of both project and the organisation, at various phases of the project life cycle	Review phased staffing and resource plans and implementation processes for various phases of the project life cycle
Reporting	Timely, relevant and reliable information is not available to support the organisation's and project's direction and decision-making processes	Reporting structures and methods are defined from the outset and assurance is obtained periodically that information reported is timely, relevant and reliable	Review PID and approved business case for reporting requirements and processes

Element 3. Risks management: management of risks and opportunities through the life cycle of the project

Area of review	Risk	Control	Audit methods include
Risk and opportunity strategy	Project risk and opportunity strategy is not consistent with the organisation's risk appetite	Risk and opportunity identification and management strategy is developed which aligns with that of organisation	Review approved business case for risk and opportunity management and processes, including fit with organisation's risk appetite and evidence of proactive risk management approach
Risk and opportunity identification, assessment and management processes	Project risks and opportunities are not identified and managed effectively	Formal risk and opportunity management processes, including formal risk register and periodic review, are implemented	Review risk and issue registers and processes for populating these Ensure that definitions of risks and issues are fully understood
Plan and implement responses to risk	Unplanned or unconsidered response to crystallisation of risk	Responsibility for action on crystallisation of risk is established, and action plan is developed	Review risk and issue processes to ensure clarity of ownership on crystallisation and ability to develop action plans

Area of review	Risk	Control	Audit methods include
Contingency	No contingency plans, processes or allowances related to occurrence of adverse events	Contingencies of time and cost form part of project planning process and approvals. As elements of plan are achieved, contingency allowances are released if unused	Assess time and cost contingency planning and processes Ensure that contingency is realistically quantified Review processes for release of contingencies
Business continuity and disaster recovery	Response to major adverse occurrence to project is unplanned or otherwise not allowed for	Business continuity plan and disaster recovery plan are established for implementation in stated circumstances. Organisation processes allow allocation of resources to mitigate and achieve delivery of continuity and recovery plans. Plans reviewed periodically	Identify role of business continuity in organisational governance and how this relates to the project governance and planning Assess extent to which plans which could affect project outcomes are reviewed periodically

Element 4. Commercial, procurement and commissioning: procurement, contract management, financial controls and engagement with commissioning processes

Area of review	Risk	Control	Audit methods include
Procurement strategy	Procurement strategy is not consistent with project and business case requirements, particularly in respect of timing and life cycle costs	Procurement strategy is agreed within business case and is consistent with organisation and project requirements	Review procurement planning processes and fit with project and organisation strategy Ensure engagement in place with organisation's procurement teams to ensure compliance with strategy
Procurement processes	Procurement processes do not comply with legal and organisational requirements and are not effectively planned and managed	Procurement processes are subject to rigorous planning, evaluation and review by both project and organisation	Review procurement processes including tendering and evaluation, to assure transparency and compliance with legal and organisational requirements

Area of review	Risk	Control	Audit methods include
Contract strategy	Contract strategy is not consistent with procurement strategy, or legal and project requirements, and may not offer value for money Contract strategy does not apportion risk to the party best able to bear it	Contract strategy should be assessed for consistency with organisation and project requirements	Assess contract strategy and planning for consistency with organisation and project requirements Assess whether contract and procurement risk is borne by the party best able to bear it, in accordance with the parties' organisational risk appetite
Contract administration	Administration of contracts does not support achievement of project objectives or does not comply with requirements of conditions of contract	Sufficient resource is available to manage and administer contracts effectively	Review procurement resource strategy at all stages of the project life cycle. Review contract administration plans
Financial control	Control of project finance and accounting matters is inadequate	Robust and effective financial control and management processes are established, including cost and cashflow reporting	Review standing financial instructions and project cost reporting procedures and processes to assess extent to which these support effective project governance
Commissioning within the organisation	Commissioning processes, reflecting the changes which will result from the project, and are to be carried out by stakeholders have not been established within the organisation	Resources, plans and equipment have been made available for training stakeholders in the changed methods of provision of services and goods which will result from introduction of the project deliverables	Review commissioning resource plans, including training and provision of suitable equipment to support changed methods of service delivery
Contract completion and handover	Project or contract is handed over or otherwise accepted and payment made although completion has not been achieved	Robust approval processes for the acceptance of contracts or projects have been established, to ensure that completion has been achieved in accordance with the conditions of contract	Review contractual approval processes to assure that projects will not be accepted nor payment made if completion has not been achieved

Element 5. Configuration management, project change controls and the PMO: processes and systems to administer and control the project and changes to it

Area of review	Risk	Control	Audit methods include
Configuration management processes	Configuration management is not effectively planned or is not consistent with the project deliverables as specified	Documented configuration management processes Responsibilities for actions assigned	Review configuration management procedures and processes, including schedule of delegation
Document management system	Document management system is not structured to support change control and configuration management processes	Planned document management system which is consistent with configuration processes and the project filing system	Review document management systems (including electronic systems) to assure effective support for project administration and governance
Scope and change management system	Changes to the baseline scope of a project may not be made in a controlled manner Project and contract changes are not effectively controlled Risk of uncontrolled scope creep	A structured and rigorous process, covering review and changes to baseline scope should be instituted	Review processes for management of changes to scope and other parameters to assure these offer effective control Review processes for managing how changes impact on programme and costs
Project filing system	Project filing system is unclear or not effectively managed and does not support the project's administration and control processes	A structured project filing system, which is consistent with organisation, project and configuration management needs is implemented	Assess project filing system (including electronic systems) to assure support for effective administration and management of the project
Project management office (PMO)	Administrative processes, as supplied through the PMO, are unsuitable, insufficient or too onerous for effective administration of project activities	A formal PMO structure, appropriate to the size and nature of the project and adequately resourced, should be established	Assess PMO structure and resourcing, to assure effective and support, scaled to the size and needs of the project
Project deliverables	There is not a process to administer achievement of deliverables	Formal processes for recording achievement of deliverables of the project and its elements are established	Review processes for recording and approving achievement of deliverables, which may be linked to contractual payment processes

Element 6. Planning and scheduling: appropriately detailed execution strategies, plans and schedules

Area of review	Risk	Control	Audit methods include
Integrated approach to planning	Planning processes are not consistent with those of the organisation or other parts of programme	Planning processes and activities are defined at high level within the organisation and with stakeholders	Assess planning processes for consistency with project and organisation requirements and with stakeholders
High level planning	There is not a high level plan in place for the whole project life cycle	Organisation board approval of high level plan and schedule through business case process

High level plan and schedule used as basis of progress and cost control and management | Review high level plan and reporting against it to organisation board

Confirm that the high level plan is regularly updated to account for changes to scope |
| Detailed planning | More detailed plans are not aligned to high level plans | Formal planning process for detailed planning held at project board level

Reconciliation process between high level and detailed plans | Assess governance arrangements for planning processes

Review detailed plan and reporting within organisation |
| Defining activities | Unclear milestones, work breakdown structure (WBS) and dates | Ensure clearly defined descriptions of deliverables and realistic plan for achievement

Reconciliation between detailed planning process and activity and resource schedules

Ensure appropriate skill level of project team (including training if required) | Assess planning, review and reporting processes to assure clarity and comprehensiveness to project team and stakeholders as required |

Area of review	Risk	Control	Audit methods include
Schedule integrity	Unrealistic assumptions made in respect of time and cost (this could be by the project team or sponsor)	Formal review of basis of planning assumptions in respect of time and cost Ensure that realistic timescales have been agreed at board level	Review basis of planning assumptions including taking expert advice to assure that those assumptions are realistic
Progress reporting	Progress reports are not provided or tailored to the appropriate level within the organisation	Appropriately detailed planning and progress reports are provided as per the project's governance structure and project assurance requirements	Assess arrangements for effective governance of project, including reporting and assurance requirements Ensure that reporting is being implemented as per the governance and assurance recommendations
Change	Project changes are made without early warning, formal documentation or clear decision-making	Change processes make provision for early warning of changes and their impacts	Assess all logs for risks, issues, actions and decisions and ensure that cost and time implications are being captured and that any significant or sensitive decisions are being recorded.
Commissioning	Requirements for new and changed service provision have not been planned for	Planning for commissioning of future service provision forms part of overall life cycle project planning	Review commissioning plans including training and resourcing, to assure fit with changed service provision Ensure that there is a process in place for continual embedding of change
Project completion and closure	Processes for completion, handover and project closure have not been planned for or are unclear	Planning for completion, handover and project closure is part of project planning process from the outset	Review approved business case and subsequent completion, handover and project closure plans and processes

Element 7. Performance and benefits management: to provide assurance that the benefits stated in the business case can be delivered within the resources made available

Area of review	Risk	Control	Audit methods include
Project benefits strategy	There is not a project benefits strategy	A benefits strategy forms part of the approved business case, and is controlled and measured against a baseline	Review approved business case for benefits strategy, and review subsequent reports against it and check that metrics are in place
Alignment of benefits with organisation strategy	Project benefits do not align with organisation strategy or objectives	Alignment of project benefits with organisation's strategy forms part of approved business case and is controlled against Continual review of business case at key project stages	Review approved business case for strategic fit of benefits Check that business case is reviewed at each project gateway
Accountability for achievement of benefits	Accountability for achievement of benefits is not allocated to the project sponsor	Project sponsor is recorded in approved business case as being accountable for achievement of benefits, and is an appropriate person to be accountable Accountability survives project completion and handover	Review approved business case and PID for governance arrangements and assess whether these are extant Assess arrangements for survival of accountability
Benefits realisation planning	No benefits realisation plan	A formal benefits realisation planning process is established, reporting to organisation and project boards	Review approved business case and assess whether a benefits realisation plan has resulted from it

Area of review	Risk	Control	Audit methods include
Measurement of benefits	Project benefits are not expressed in measurable form	Project benefits are expressed in measurable form which can be baselined Performance is tracked against benefits realisation plan Benefits realisation measurement continues throughout the project life cycle and appropriate action taken to preserve and continue to embed benefits as required	Review approved business case and benefits realisation plan for extent of measurable benefits, where these are consistent with the project objectives Review if the project is able to demonstrate that it is delivering both outputs and outcomes (achievement of benefits realisation)
Benefits realisation review and post-project evaluation	Provision not made to review benefits realisation nor to evaluate project performance	Benefits realisation review is planned for from the outset, based on approved business case Post-project evaluations are planned from the outset to take place at appropriate times, particularly before the project team is broken up	Review approved business case for provision for benefits realisation planning and management Review if resource is in place to ensure that benefits realisation plan can be properly implemented Assess arrangements for post-project evaluations and legacy learning (where appropriate). Such arrangements should be consistent with commercial confidentiality requirements of the organisation Assess that project has a plan for managing transition to 'business-as-usual' to ensure that benefits are not lost'

Element 8. Stakeholder management and communications: all stakeholders affected by the project have been identified and are appropriately involved

Area of review	Risk	Control	Audit methods include
Stakeholder management strategy	A stakeholder management strategy has not been established	A stakeholder management strategy forms part of the approved business case, ensuring due consideration is given to the requirements of all stakeholders Ensure sufficient resource in place to delivery stakeholder management strategy	Review approved business case for stakeholder management strategy requirements, and assess resulting processes and activities Review that sufficient resource is in place to address stakeholder management
Communication strategy	A communication strategy has not been established	A communications strategy is established, to take account of the need for all stakeholders to be informed to the necessary extent	Review approved business case for communications strategy requirements and assess resulting processes and activities
Identification of stakeholders	Not all stakeholders have been identified	Stakeholders mapped to record levels of influence, interest and involvement, and capacity to disrupt progress	Review stakeholder management plan for mapping processes and completeness Review process for managing most influential/interested stakeholders
Stakeholder management plan	Stakeholder interests are not identified	Stakeholder management plan established Policies to engage stakeholders commensurate with their needs are established Regular reporting to stakeholders	Review stakeholder management plan and subsequent reports for policies and activities to engage stakeholders
Communication plan	There is not a structured communications framework and plan for the project	Communications structure and plan established to define communication requirements for the project and organisation and how these will be distributed	Review communications plan and subsequent reports for policies and actions to communicate with stakeholders and others

Area of review	Risk	Control	Audit methods include
Integration with contractors' communications strategies and plans	Undesirable release or retention of project information	Agreed protocols for contractors' communications form part of contractual documentation. Joint communications plan developed, to be operated under control of project manager	Review contractual documents to assess extent and consistency of protocols between contracting parties on communication. Review joint communications plan and its governance arrangements

Element 9. Organisational capability and culture: people, behaviours, teams, processes, systems and the working environment including the organisation's culture

Area of review	Risk	Control	Audit methods include
People and staffing	Project staff resource requirements are unplanned	Project staffing plan is established as part of approved business case, and achievement is reported to organisation and project boards	Review approved business case and PID to assure staffing plan has been established and is reported on under governance arrangements
Teamwork	Teams are not integrated sufficiently to support project and organisation objectives	Emphasis by project manager on ensuring staff resources form effective teams whose performance is subject to review	Discuss with project manager the structure and performance of the project team(s), and roles and responsibilities
Culture	Project or contractor culture does not align with that of organisation	Integrated culture requirements statement forms part of business case or cultural expectations included in contractual documents	Review approved business case and contractual documents for details of cultural arrangements including governance arrangements

Area of review	Risk	Control	Audit methods include
Processes and systems	Processes and systems in operation do not enhance delivery or deliverability of project and its benefits	Review of all systems to ensure flexible flow is maintained and disruption to achievement of objectives is minimised	Discuss with project management and review to assure flexibility is maintained and disruption caused by inappropriate systems is minimised
Working environment	Suitable premises/locations to work from for effective delivery are not supplied or otherwise are not available for staff and other resources	Requirement for suitable working environment/s in appropriate locations to be stated in business case and in contractual documents as necessary Compliance with statutory and other requirements assessed End of project release of accommodation and facilities planned from the outset	Review approved business case and PID for provision being made in respect of suitable working environment and accommodation, in conjunction with review of staffing and other project resource plans
Leadership	Unidentified or ineffective project leadership does not allow project and its staff to flourish	Leadership assessment audits, related to the outcomes of project assurance activities, should be instigated to improve performance of project management and staff Ensure sponsor and board fully understand their project roles	Review outcomes of leadership assessment audits and subsequent actions, to assess how performance of project management is improving
Administrative and IT resources	Administrative and IT services, software and equipment do not effectively support delivery of the project objectives	Provision of effective administrative and IT resources forms part of approved business case Available administrative and IT resources are subject to review, with the object of best supporting achievement of project objectives	Review approved business case and PID, to assess extent to which administrative and IT resources have been provided, and are subject to review

Element 10. Social responsibility and sustainability: managing the impact of project delivery on the social, physical, ecological and economic environment including health and safety

Area of review	Risk	Control	Audit methods include
Social responsibility and risks	Project scope, delivery and benefits are not aligned with the organisation's reputational risk or social responsibility appetite	Organisation board should assess reputational risks to the organisation during the process of approving the business case Project-related reputational risk should be placed on the organisations risk register and be subject to review as required	Assess consideration by organisation board during approval of business case process Review organisation risk register for project-related potential causes of reputational risk
Health, safety and security	Health, safety and security management systems have not been developed or implemented	Health, safety and security requirements are subject of a comprehensive management plan, progress against which is reported to organisation and project boards	Review health safety and security planning processes, and subsequent reports to organisation and project boards

Appendix 2

Comparison of project audit elements for review, with assurance measures toolkit categories

(see para 2.2.1)

Project audit elements

Element	Description	Comparable toolkit criteria – ref:
1	Project definition and requirements management – clear and controlled baseline requirements, objectives, success criteria, business case, terms of reference, contracts and benefits realisation.	1 Client and scope
2	Project organisation and governance – the processes to align the interests and strategic direction of sponsors and stakeholders.	10 Governance
3	Risks management – management of risks and opportunities through the life cycle of the project.	2 Risks and opportunities
4	Commercial, procurement and commissioning management – procurement and contract management, financial controls and engagement with commissioning processes.	5 Supply chain
5	Configuration management, project and change controls and PMO – processes and systems to administer and control the project and changes to it.	6 Solution
6	Project planning and scheduling – appropriately detailed execution strategies, plans and schedules.	3 Planning and scheduling
7	Performance and benefits management – to provide assurance that the benefits stated in the business case can be delivered within the resources made available.	9 Performance

Element	Description	Comparable toolkit criteria – ref:
8	Stakeholder management and communications – all stakeholders affected by the project have been identified and are appropriately involved.	1 Client and scope; 10 Governance
9	Organisational capability and culture – people, behaviours, teams and the working environment including the organisation's culture.	4 Organisational capability and culture
10	Social responsibility and sustainability – managing the impact of project delivery on the social, physical, ecological and economic environment including health and safety.	8 Social responsibility and sustainability

Toolkit criteria

Criteria	Description
1	Client and scope – clear and controlled baseline requirements, objectives, success criteria, business case, terms of reference, contracts and benefits realisation.
2	Risks and opportunities – management of risk and opportunity through the life cycle of the project.
3	Planning and scheduling – appropriately detailed execution strategies, plans and schedules.
4	Organisational capability and culture – people, behaviours, teams, processes, systems and the working environment.
5	Supply chain – procurement processes, engagement with, and capability of, both the internal and external supply chain.
6	Solution – the deliverables and outcomes that meet the client requirements. This includes product and/or service quality and the impact of the finished product or service on the social, physical and economic environment.
7	Finance – commercial management and administration.
8	Social responsibility and sustainability – managing the impact of project delivery on the social, physical, ecological and economic environment; this includes health and safety.
9	Performance – measuring all facets of performance against the baseline requirements, variance analysis and management action.
10	Governance – the processes to align the interests and strategic direction of sponsors and stakeholders.

Criteria are taken from the APM publication, *Measures for Assuring Projects: APM Toolkit* (2016)